Conversations *with a* River

Poems by

Annie Prescott

Blessings!
Annie Prescott
2022

Anniemara

1258 Riverside Avenue

Somerset, MA 02726

www.anniemara.com

ISBN 979-8-9866437-1-7 (Paperback)

ISBN 979-8-9866437-0-0 (e-book)

Art by Annie Prescott

Book design by Barbara Aronica-Buck

Cover design by Keith Conforti

Printed in the United States of America

This collection is lovingly dedicated to my husband, Frank Prescott. He has unfailingly provided me with love and encouragement in pursuing my dreams and continues to open doors to what seems to be impossible.

Frank, 2020

Today is your birthday.
You are a 76'er!
How I love you,
your kindness and calm.
You are interested in everything I do,
offering patience and support.
You have given me the opportunities,
the means and the reasons to create.
No tortured artist am I,
thriving on your gifts of space,
ideas and plans.
A listener, a quiet dependable constant,
You are also irreverent, stubborn,
and completely politically incorrect.
You have the most beautiful blue eyes
I have ever seen.

My Love Affair with Somerset

Who am I?

My name is Annie,
but it was not always so.
I have been Ann Marie,
sometimes Annmarie
or AMC
I have always been ReeRee
because Ann Marie was hard
for small lips to shape.
I will always be ReeRee
but I became Annie slowly,
when I finally found my art.
Now I create magical birds
and fish and faeries and gnomes.
I am clothed in color and layers of clay.
Now my hands are callused and cracked
my body complaining in cold or heat.
But my soul?
My soul is soaring
and I splash out with joyful abandon.
Ann Marie learned.
ReeRee nurtured
and Annie dances with
waving arms, rolling hips
and flying feet.
My favorite number is three,
and I rejoice in my many names.

I am . . .

About to leave my sixties,
but the desire for re-invention is strong.
There is something to be said
about experiencing the wonders
and the mysteries of my little life.
Sometimes I feel so joyful
I can hardly stop myself
from dancing.
Even old bones can turn a jig.
But then there are those other moments
when my mind is numb from feeling so much pain.
When memories roll over me like
waves in a storm,
and I no longer have an anchor.
Then I know that great joy and
great pain are not so very far apart.
I feel them both much more vividly
now that I am no longer young.
I try not to let my life
be ruled by sudden storms.
You know, the ones that come out of nowhere,
angry and hissing,
pummeling the plants and roiling the river;
turning day into a gray, swollen darkness,
pulling branches and leaves from the gentle trees.
Nature is cruel as well as kind,
and its fury must come to an end.
Gratefully I pick up the pieces
and slowly start again.

Irony

Although I am growing older,
I seem to be getting younger!
I desire my days to be simple & kind,
and my nights to be dreamfree & starlit.
My heart is etched with tiny cracks
as those I love create new homes in my soul.
My thoughts are often filled with wonder
about bird songs and anchored, ancient trees.
I, myself, am rooted but stretching toward heaven.
Each day becomes an unpromised gift to be celebrated and sung.
I'm not worried about tomorrow,
I only have my now.
I am stronger, though my body weakens,
and wiser as I forget tiny details.
What a beautiful irony to gain so much as I lose . . .

January 4th – Cape Cod

A sunburst sparkle on the salt marsh;
the air is bitter cold, the sand
like fractured fragments of glass beneath my feet,
and the silence –
whispers of winter against the wind.
It is January 4th,
my 70th birthday.
I am younger than I was yesterday,
and my soul is dancing.

Sky Blue Pink

Gramma Anna –The sunrise is your favorite color, sky blue pink,
just like the First Communion dress
you described to me on the bus
on the way to the city.
Of course, it was just a magical,
mosaic piece of the dreams we put together,
knowing that white was the only acceptable choice.
But I squeezed my eyes shut,
and for a moment I was beautiful,
wearing colors only fairies could weave;
a gift from you to me.

My Totem

There is a red fox living in my yard,
and he dances around in his black stocking feet
in the pre-dawn stillness.
If I am very quiet, I can watch him
leaving footprints in the frosty glass shards,
and they look like bread crumbs guiding his way home.
One day, he suddenly turned, his large black shoe button eyes
focused on mine.
He never blinked, but suddenly, joyfully, howled a song
of freedom.
He shook his auburn winter coat, and then he was simply gone.

Change?

I never tire of change.
I am only a work in progress.
When I think I am finished,
the bottom falls out,
and once again, I am adrift
in these whimsical waves of change.
So I paint the scene over again,
sometimes with a shaking hand.
Of course, a new painting emerges,
totally different with colors and lines,
a new, uncertain idea that will
change as I change,
knowing, of course, that enough
Will never be enough.

Before Dawn . . .

I seem to slowly inch forward
only to double back,
hiding in the haven of memories.
The future is so very risky,
not to mention unknown and uncertain.
But there is a single, silent star
winking at me in the dawnlight,
daring me to make one more wish,
take one more chance
become the observed rather than the observer.

Day's End

A day must end in order to begin again.
I think about this when darkness descends.
As the sun surrenders to the inky sky,
the quiet time begins.
I always hope I will find the stars
winking and ready for wishing.
Everything living can rest now,
wrapped in a blanket of peaceful hope
that the world will be kinder tomorrow.

September 11, 2001

When there is no other way
To rationalize reality
I am left with the fact
That evil really does exist.
On a brilliant blue September morning,
So much crashed into smokey pieces,
Scattered, torn and tangled on the smoldering streets
Sky-high dreams became the stuff of nightmares,
in less time than a tear drops.
Much more collapsed than buildings.
Much more exploded than planes.
As sirens shrieked and the sky grew dark in the billowing
blackness of acrid dust,
an anguished cry echoed through
the vast cement forest,
and a wounded, aching heart
stirred beneath the rubble . . .

A Storm Blessing, Sunday, August 22

I am so very, very grateful
for my cottage on the river,
for my studio cluttered with creativity,
ever so close to the rolling waves;
for my fearless friend, King Gull,
enthroned on his seaweed strewn rock;
for my wind chimes, dancing despite the storm.
I am grateful for my bird feeder families,
the mourning doves and their children,
the cardinal, the chickadees, and, yes,
even those ill-tempered blue jays...
for the ground hog, tunneled under the deck
and the bold cottontail rabbits relishing the bruised crabapples.
I gaze at the sometimes star-sprinkled sky
and the August Sturgeon full moon
casting a magical path across the water.
Most of all I am grateful for my sense of wonder in the
tiniest acorn and the mightiest pine
a blessing sings deep in my soul. . . .
I am so very, very grateful.

Very First Day of School

Once
I was a chubby, bespectacled, pigtailed
student in a blue plaid dress,
saddle shoes and ribbons.
I clutched books that I had chosen
And would now learn to read;
the gift of a patient, nameless, remarkable teacher
clothed in black from head to toe.
The world began to blossom on that day.
As my left-hand brushed the pages,
I plunged into a magical, mysterious, magnificent place
Of shining hallways
and endless circular stairways.
I made my way wading
Through leaf-strewn hidden paths
and never once looked back.
I was perched on seven hills
And my wings flew open.

Captain

My dog, Captain, was never a good boy.
He roamed the neighborhood,
always looking for trouble.
Chasing cars and especially motorcycles,
he scattered our neighbor's chickens,
demolishing a fragile fence.
In games of hide and seek, he always gave us away,
barking at streetlights, calling us home.
He shunned his kibble and ate with the family,
destroying Christmas cupcakes and stealing
sizzling hot dogs from the grill.
When we raced into the river, he was right beside us,
joyously shaking his fur and rolling in the sand.
Loyal to a fault, he never left us alone.
Sprawled out on the sofa, a snoring storm,
dreaming of morning mischief and mayhem.
No, Captain was never a good boy,
but his battle-scarred face was full of love
and his heart was as big as the sky.

Dunkin

Our cat Dunkin
is an ancient gray-haired man.
He patrols our house at night
and curls into a ball of sleep when morning spreads open.
He finds the sun path stretching across the cottage floor,
and his old limbs drink in the daylight.
It is true that he loves Frank a lot,
and me just a little.
But I don't mind.
I watch him stare at the bird feeder,
lost in memories of more adventurous days.
His eyes reflect the cold pull of many winters
and the soft buttery springtime sun.
True, his years are many, but he is peaceful and so content.
He roams about, a mighty, ageless warrior
until he finds his food dish empty . . .

The Field

At the foot of Buckner Court,
near the Moquin's house,
a stone wall separated civilization
and the field.
Climbing the wall was easy
and the reward was our own private kingdom.
Venturing down a path, perhaps prepared by
other children long since grown,
I saw my first tad poles in a tiny pond
we suddenly came upon.
They were swimming in schools like tiny shadows.
We climbed a great rock
a glacier gift from ancient days.
We christened it "Bonnie's Bum,"
a dubious tribute to a sometimes playmate.
We gathered Queen Anne's Lace and marveled
at its intricate lacy beauty.
We picked berries that would be devoured
later drowned in cream and sugar.
It's all disappeared now, the wall, the rock, the pond.
Replaced by copy-cat houses and paved streets.
There's a small patch surrounded by highway,
but still unkempt in a wild tangle of trees.
I dream of it at night.

The Poplars

The first time I saw you,
I knew we were moving to a castle,
with graceful white columns
and overgrown, tangled sunken gardens.
There were quince trees and grape arbors;
paths of brick weaving through the yard.
There was an old barn with horse stalls and stairs leading to
nowhere in the dappled sunlight.
There was a wooden well
and an outhouse set back in sprawling lilacs and forsythia.
Best of all, there was a cupola at the very top of my castle
with windows in every direction.
I could look out over the river until it bent toward the ocean,
just as a sea captain's wife did awaiting the wooden sailing ship
arriving home.
What a gift it was for me,
growing up in the gentle, benign shadows of the past
while waiting to wrap my arms around the mighty future.

Village Kids

Although I lived in the Village,
I was never a village kid.
I went to school in the city,
and that made me an outsider.
My sisters and brother were village bred,
and they navigated the streets
of the oldest part of town.
In the summer, I was a loner,
gone again in the fall.
I rode the bus with other village deserters.
And I knew the city better than the town.
The kids in the Village never rode buses,
they walked in patrols
down the crooked hill
until they reached the penny candy store,
jutting out over the river.
I never saw a penny candy counter in the city.

The SHA Christmas Play

Every year we marched up the leaf-strewn street
to the high school auditorium.
We were armed with assignments and roles to play;
a dancing bear with a jaunty red bow,
a weatherman in an oiled yellow slicker,
a lollipop seller with a loaded tray.
I always hoped for a coveted spot
in the still-life Nativity,
the annual curtain closer.
But, it just wasn't meant to be.
So I happily caroled from one chorus to the next,
soaking up the spirit of the season.
And when we reached that final frost-filled night
when it all came together,
I knew we were shining as brightly
as the star-splattered sky.
And my parents always clapped the loudest.

Meet Me at the Marsh

Flooding the Marsh was a welcome event,
firming the fact
that the gray days were gathering,
and it was skating weather.
Plans were passed,
blades were sharpened,
hot chocolate steamed on the stove.
We doubled our socks and gloves,
and breathed in the perfume of
pine wood camp fires across the lot.
When the challenge was spoken
we raced for the mother rock,
a ghostly, glacial gift looming large.
We tangled with the marsh grass,
gliding past nets and scraping hockey sticks.
Red-cheeked and dreaming of dancing on ice,
we feasted on frigid air
for a few precious hours
until darkness deepened and called us home.

Walking on Riverside

It's a well-travelled , tangled road
that runs beside the river;
shared by walkers,
runners and pets.
If you look hard enough
you'll see the fidddlehead ferns
forcing their faces through ice-caked snow,
hardy harbingers of the still sleeping spring.
The swans are circling the sheltering cove
travelling by twos through the marshy grasses,
surrounded by grey geese skidding
to a stop along the river's edge.
If you are truly blessed and very lucky
you'll spy a seal sunning on the ragged rocks;
but that is a special gift,
never to be taken for granted.
Still, the river and the road
remain best friends
winding their way toward home.

The Fiddlehead Ferns

It's not easy to spot the Fiddlehead Ferns
although they love to nestle near the water.
If you walk along Riverside,
chances are you will spot them
gracefully bowing to the sea grass
as the wind invites them to dance.
Their tenure is brief
but ever so joyful
and filled with the celebration of spring,
each one an amazing maze
of curling wonder.

The Village Library

At least once a week
I walked up the unpaved lane
and onto High Street,
past the marsh and the
wintertime skaters.
There was the Village School
on one side of the street
and the library on the other.
Painted clapboard white,
it was not a very imposing
building at all.
But when I went through
the door,
it was a castle, a forest,
sometimes a city.
Polished floors and tables,
shelf after shelf of books
waiting to transport me
to another time, another country,
another planet.

The stern-faced librarian
would reward me
with a ghost of a smile.
Sometimes
I would simply gaze
out the reference room window,
at the unspoiled landscape of fields
and trees.
It's all gone now,
the school, the trees and especially
the library.
I do still find books and
lose myself in their magic
but I ache for that kingdom
beyond the heavy glass doors

Downtown at Christmastime

Because my school
is on the seven hills,
walking downtown in winter
is not so simple,
especially since I have traded
my serviceable saddle shoes
for more glamorous penny loafers.
But when I do reach Main Street
the spell of the season
swirls all around me.
I seek out the silver tree
that transforms the front
of the largest store.
My father strung the lights
from one end of Main Street
to the other.
And he reminded us every year.
I drink in the scents of the season,
grilled hamburgers from Harry's
and Woolworth's roasted nuts.
Finally, I warm my hands
against the cup of that most wonderful
winter remedy,
a steaming cup of coffee at Van Dyke's counter,
right near the wooden pickle barrel.
Far too soon, I must catch
the 5:15 bus
in front of the library's granite steps
and I gaze back once more at Dad's
twinkling star lights
on one of the shortest days of the year.

The Memorial Day Parade

Every year we faithfully practiced our marching
on the pavement surrounding the American Legion Hall.
White gloves and creased sashes, we were ready to honor
those warriors who never returned from battle.
I always carried the flag, leading the troops of Girl Scouts
in green, well-spaced waves
along County Street festooned in red, white and blue.
We prayed for sunny weather and the town cheered us on,
sitting in lawn charirs along the route.
And so proudly they came
the Gold Star mothers,
the High School marching band,
the town dignitaries stepping smartly
as we turned down Center Street,
So full of pride, hope and the bittersweet pull of time gone by.
The wreathes were reverently placed at each memorial.
A distant bugle blew Taps, the saddest song in the world.
And then there were donuts at the VFW, a reward for a job well
done, before we all scurried off to sing the songs of summer.

Wilbur's on the Taunton

My mother would sometimes get a twinkle in her eye as she
hummed her way though her daily chores.
She was in another place then,
and I so wanted her to share it.
"I saw Glenn Miller at Wilbur's"
and she would begin the story I loved to hear.
"It was a starlit night on the Taunton River." The Wilbur twinkled
like a Christmas tree, beckoning everyone to come and dance.
People gathered around outside sharing excited staccato greetings.
The perfumed, perfectly coifed women and the slicked back,
cigarette smoking men paraded by one another as they waited to
enter the hall.
And inside, the band was pumping,
pulsing horns and dangerous drums.
The crowded floor was a smoke filled mirage of dancers and
drinkers,
punctuated by servers bearing trays of cocktails weaving their way
through the throbbing maze.

"Glenn Miller looked right at me,"
she shyly and proudly admitted.
"But my eyes were on your Dad.
I fell in love that night, intoxicated by the music and cheap
cologne.
We whirled until we were breathless
working our way out to the silence of the river."
"What happened then?" I eagerly asked.
"Then?" she replied.
"That is a story for another day.
It's getting time for dinner."
And the spell would be broken,
although I swear I could still hear
the fading flourish of the trumpet's solo
wafting across the water.

The Somerset Council Oak
How did this happen?

With branches embracing the sky and roots carving
through the clay,
stretching and curving through the earth.
The proud Council oak seemed timeless.
It provided the shade for ancient treaties to be signed,
grievances voiced and problems solved.
It marked the center of our own little universe with a sweeping,
majestic dignity.
Birds constructed fragile nests
in the protection of its leafy boughs
Yes, it was steadfast, dependable, constant.
But it came crashing down in the springtime wind,
in spite of the tiny leaf buds that were valiantly trying to bloom.
Somehow, this oak knew that it had completed its purpose.
It called out to those who would bless it with their songs and
smudge sticks.
And they came, one last time, to gratefully guide it home,
thankful for a life so well lived
And reminding us that nothing stays forever,
so dig in and bloom as long as you can.

My Back Yard – The Taunton River

My Reliable Friend

The river always recognizes me,
although I have left for long periods of time.
I etched waves on my arm without
knowing why I needed them.
But the river is patient.
And when I finally come home,
it smooths my jagged edges
and subtly shows me the way
to follow the curve of the shore.

My Morning Song

As I watch the fire of the rising sun,
I am singing my morning song.
I'm so very glad to be here,
greeting my river,
as it waves back to me.
How wonderful,
to be given another chance
to create something magical;
to sing with my faithful bird friends,
to splash bright paint
on an empty canvas.
The morning has such a sweet scent.
It is all about beginning.
I will not think of endings,
they always take care of themselves.
So I sing, as the sun sparkles
in my eyes,
a song of thanksgiving for the
gift of now.

A Whisper of Change

I heard the river gently whisper
that winter was waiting in the winds
with a somber step,
after the riotous dance of the autumn.
Soft shadows are muting the sun
And there's a misty mirror on the water.
There's a crunch in my footsteps
as I walk the frost filled path.
"Don't be sad," counseled the river.
"It's time to turn within,
to find the secret spot of warmth
deep in the ember's glow.
So celebrate the changeable landscape,
the rhythm-filled heart of your soul".

Early Morning

When the morning mist
mingles with the river,
it turns into silvery smoke
snaking across the still water.
It really only lasts for moments,
as if it knows that the day is impatient to begin.
The sun yawns its way across the
pale, gray sky,
and the darkness disappears
for a while.

Fog vs. Mist

I never confuse the morning mist with fog.
A misty morning quenches the still sleeping earth
with a life-giving tonic of wonder and growth.
But fog only hides the river
settling like a shroud of chilly misery.
The dew drop mist is playful.
Now you see it; now you don't.
Fog is so heavy in a gloomy mystery
and so stubbornly slow to take its leave.
Morning mist?
It sings and dances in diamonds
on the grass,
until in a final, spectacular sparkle
the newborn day awakens.

The Journey

In the not quite light, the river shimmers,
touching the well-worn rocks lining the shoreline.
Partners in an infinite dance,
they are ever faithful to one another,
never doubting the wisdom of an age-old journey,
as they push against the sea wall
and then gently recede.
The final destination is the sea,
a mother patiently waiting
for her wayward children.
But there is no hurry.
There is no doubt, or fear, and certainly no regret
for that which is left behind.
There is only the grand adventure of now,
traveling with the tides.

Constant Contest

It takes place every morning,
in the cove beneath my window.
The gulls and the geese converse across the frosty dawn.
Their calls are imperative but not alarming;
simple, singsong statements about the sunrise on the river.
At times, it becomes contentious cackling, as the daylight brushes
away the dark.
It's time to glide with the tide,
To fly in formation,
To forage for food;
a morning blessing from the river.

Poem 12/4/2020

The waves of my river rise
and then fall again;
waves of sparkling joy
and waves of darkest sorrow;
waves of crystalline peace
and waves of foaming discord;
waves that gently caress my feet,
and waves that hurtle over me until I am knocked down.
They will not fail to return,
although I will.
They will continue to kiss the river rocks,
which are worn but steadfast.

Waves (part 2)
Why do they say a wave breaks?
This is so not true.
A wave encompasses;
it soothes, it spreads.
It surrounds the aching shore,
bringing it comfort,
drenching its dryness,
leaving it glistening and refreshed.
But does a wave break?
I hardly think so.

A Conversation with a Friend

My one purpose, said the river, is to reach the endless ocean.
So I pull out the tide and then push it back in again.
I sculpt my shores and trickle down to tiny brooks
that curl and swirl over my ancient stones.
I whirl with my partner, the wind,
And become a crystalline glass in the moon's mirror.
I gently kiss the land and then drench it with my
life-affirming spray.
I lovingly carry my sea birds, my river dwellers,
anyone who needs my strength.
I am softer than the sea but it needs me
to make this journey and I do it with joy.
Never forget that it is a wonderful gift to be needed.
"What an unbelievable responsibility,"
I said to my friend.
"I wish I were more like you."
and the river chuckled.
"You think too much...just live in the moment
and always try to be necessary."

An Observation about the River

The river sings with the song of the sea gull.
They are, after all, sisters,
celebrating each day in the joyous company of one another.
The river's bubbling laugh soothes the wave-tumbled rocks,
bathing them in sun sparkle in an infinite dance.
The river sings in the gentle breeze of springtime,
an ancient hymn of praise and perserverance;
a tune that changes as it ebbs and flows.
It is true that sometimes the river does weep for
days long gone by,
for memories that are tattered and torn.
This river has witnessed so much,
winding with the shoreline, changing with the tide.
But its journey is an endless one,
searching for the mother sea.
It always does what it was meant to do,
nourishing all that it touches.

Gray days

It's hard to conjure up gray days
when the winking holiday lights are
dancing across the crystal frost
scattering darkness in a star-filled sky.
But beautiful baubles cannot last long,
and the river wraps itself in a cloak of gray.
Storm clouds tumble upon one another
in an effort to cover the sun.
The time has come for a winter sleep,
for burrowing down against the ground
next to the seeds of Spring's return.

Sun-day

The early morning sunshine
has cast a path upon my river,
beckoning me with its bubbling babble.
This day is so very new;
pristine in its presence,
filled with precious promise.
The darkness that blanketed my eyes
has finally fled, safely sleeping in the soft clay.
Morning is a blank canvas
waiting to receive splashes of riotous color.
I have been given the gift of another day.
I pray that I use it well.

Samhain + the Full Blue Moon
October 31, 2020

On the sacred celebration of Samhain
the full blue moon turned night to day,
carving a glistening path on the river,
leading right to my doorstep.
It boldly beckoned me to come out
from behind the veil of too many tears.
This night was meant for dancing,
for waving my arms and surrendering my sadness.
There is no time for hesitating.
The clouds will soon return,
and the dance will be finished

Out of the Darkness

The river had a gossamer, gloomy grayness that morning;
the snow began to fall.
Dancing and darting across the dock, it soon settled in.
This was no ordinary storm, but a breathing blizzard,
frosting the beach with marshmallow dollops,
cloaking the somber, skeletal trees in the softest ermine.
The sea gulls drifted downwind, unconcerned about nature's roaring wrath.
The river waves frothed and foamed, spewing icy shards of frost.
Danger outweighed beauty as the landscape disappeared,
creating a new world of peaks and valleys.
Finally, darkness descended.
The wind began to whisper.
A lone star tremulously tried to twinkle,
and the waning crescent moon softly sparkled the snow.

A Christmas Week Message from the River

I heard the whisper in the wind
as it white-capped the river.
You cannot fight the tide
or the phases of the moon.
You cannot stop the seasons.
The beginnings, the endings as well.
Take a lesson from the sea gulls.
They simply ride the wind
They never struggle.
The storms will always be sudden,
fierce and frightening
but they will eventually give way
to the holiness of hope.
You have but one chance to live,
so take it.

New Year's Message from the River

This year, my plan is to
glide with the wind that
suddenly rises on the river,
just as the sea gulls do.
They refuse to struggle
against the storm,
but ride above the white capped waves
until the sky is clear.
Then, slowly, they pick their path
among the river rocks.
They are somewhat bruised and breathless
but very far from broken.

January

One bitterly cold January morning
the geese assembled on the frost-filled river.
I counted 87 of them, as well as a sprinkling of mallards
and a lone buffalo head duck.
Squawking and honking, they drifted close to the dock,
eager to share their agenda.
"Why are you here?" I asked them,
as they noisily debated, trying to out honk one another.
"Why are you not someplace warm and sunny, where you can flap
your wings and bask for a while?"
But they were much too busy to answer,
honking out plans and possibilities.
As quickly as it had begun, it was over.
They floated into formation
and drifted downriver.
But they left me with a gift,
letting me know that they were wintering with me;
there was no thought of leaving.

The King and his Lady

The sea gull king returned today,
assuming his throne upon the river rocks.
But he was not alone.
The gray crone perched by his side,
looking weathered and weary,
sitting stooped in her solitude.
She was as close to the king as air,
and she touched him with her worn wing,
affirming her affection.
She is bedraggled and battle scarred
while the king is strong and sure of himself.
Yet he knows that his crone is beautiful.
He treasures each of her fragmented feathers
as they lean together
to drink in the day.

Advice from King Seagull #1

Alone is not the same as lonely.
The King seagull taught me that
as he balanced on his seaweed-strewn throne.
Standing between the river and the sky,
he stands strong, sighs and sings
his prayer of protection.
His faith and freedom incantation
is meant to be heard by my seeking soul.
He shares as he would with any fellow
tenant of this earth.
A seasoned traveler, he know that the
journey must ultimately be taken alone
although there can be so many guides
along the way.
And then he is gone.

Ichabod the Crane

He balances on one leg,
as thin as the waving reeds by the river.
He's staring at something I cannot see.
He seems so fragile, so far away from home;
a silent sentinel at river's edge.
Finally,
he spreads his white wings
and stretches across the sky,
fragility forgotten.

Advice from the River

Only the river
can soften the edges
of my storm-weary soul.
And it always reminds me
that I am stronger this season
in spite of the loss of light
and the last echoes of laughter.
You see, the river only recognizes
the newness of things.
It has no time for yesterday
and no fear of tomorrow.
It is content with the rising
and falling of the tide
and the waxing and waning of
the moon.
Only the river can reassure
me that the dance will continue
although the partners will change.

Turning the Wheel of the Year

September

The sun seems older in September
and more careworn than it was in May.
The long, luxurious days are over,
and there's an almost imperceptible
chill before dawn.
It is too soon for autumn
to spread its jeweled cloak.
But it's too late for fireflies
and lazy walks along the river.
Now is the in-between time.
The sun will be slow to surrender,
but there is a whisper in the wind.
It caresses the last plants of summer
and bids them to welcome change.

September 30, 2020

And so,
September will exit the stage today,
carrying its birthdays and beach days.
The first day of school has come and gone,
as well as the first day of Autumn.
But it is not leaving quietly,
as windswept rain rails against
the wind chimes.
The white capped waves on the river
offer a silent salute.
It is so very familiar with endings
as well as beginnings.
It always welcomes both.
Unfazed by the morning's rainy rage,
it continues on its way.

Almost Autumn

I am ready for the fire of autumn.
I have been too long in the sun.
I'm craving clear, cool nights
and misty, magic mornings.
I'm searching for sunflowers, sweaters,
and scarlet leaves.
Cranberries, candles and burnt orange pumpkins
decorate my table
in anticipation of the quiet time,
just ahead of the darkness.

When Mother Nature is Angry

Summertime does bring those sudden downpours.
Almost without warning, a blistering
rain hits the hot pavement
with smoke and sizzle.
Little rivers magically appear,
as the parched brook becomes
bloated and furious.
The wind is so full of itself,
it doesn't take prisoners but
revels in destruction.
Mother Nature has lost her patience
with those determined to desecrate her world.
She shouts until exhausted,
remembering that she does love these wayward children.
A few streets over, the sun beams again
on the sparkling broken branches
scattered everywhere

The Forecast is for Rain

It will rain today for sure.
The sunrise as much as told me so.
The heavy gray clouds will collide until they cry.
And the last of the snow cover will surrender.
The road will glisten with diamond drops.
The sleeping seedlings will embrace wet earth.
The river will wait as it always does,
until the next sunrise speaks.

Rain on October 13

A quiet rain is dropping through the darkness
of not quite dawn.
It's rhythm is a soft staccato.
No slicing shards shatter the pavement.
This rain is soothing, almost a hymn
rolling over the still green leaves,
mending the cracks in parched pathways,
weaving itself among the reaching roots
of the ancient pine.

Always about Autumn

The change is ever so subtle.
It begins in a breeze that no longer speaks of summer,
As the leaves, once so grassy green
draw up a rusty blanket to cover the earth.
Soon they will crunch their way
into the still warm soil
with a promise to feed the seeds and roots
that are waiting for them.
They will appear again in the hopeful
promise of spring
but now it is time to rest a while
as the guardian trees stand watch.
Dream of dappled sunshine darting
across your upturned face.
Breathe softly until spring beckons you upwards.

The Rose Café, November 5, 2020

I drove through a rainswept parking lot
next to the Rose Café.
The pavement was strewn with
freshly fallen leaves
and a forlorn pumpkin stood by the doorway.
I seemed a million miles away from
the hectic hospital across the street,
where the wail of an ambulance
has ruined someone's plans.
The café was shuttered and locked,
and my disappointment diffused
through the orange-yellow curtain of leaves.
I could still smell the scent of spices leftover
from lunch time.
Looking down, I saw one perfectly
formed oak leaf.
But I did not pick it up.
I knew it had a life as well as I had one.
As I got back in my car, it began to rain again.

The Changing Time

When the wind becomes a bluster
instead of a breeze,
and the fire of the sun
becomes the glow of the hearth;
when the river rears back
and slams the shore
it has caressed all summer,
the changing time is upon us.
This is not the time for wanderlust,
or for unexplored pathways.
Chilly breaths beckon us home.
The barn doors are closed,
the harvest safely stowed away.
It's time to gather the crunching leaves
letting them mingle with the still warm
but sleepy earth.
We will meet them again in
the faraway blossoms of spring.
But now it is the changing time,
and the earth is ready for a rest.

First Frost

Although I knew it was overdue,
the first frost startled me
when it breathed an icy blanket
across the yard.
The sun awakened to a magical,
crystal kingdom of sharp
shards of frozen dew.
A mist swirled up from the river
in a ghost-like delicate dance.
The tiny bittersweet berry branches
became glowing rubies for one last day.
I saw the footprints of the red
fox etched in the grass as he
scurried to his leaf-lined borough.
Overhead, the shadowed snow geese
squawked their leaving song.
I started thinking of wood fires,
extra blankets,
and gentle, healing sleep.

Winter Solstice 2021

Silver snow,
silver sky,
silver settling on the river.
This is my holiest time of the year.
And when the darkness does descend
ending this shortest of days,
all of God's creatures
will sigh and softly sleep,
as silver stars timelessly turn the wheel.

Godspeed

The wild geese are leaving.
I saw them last night, silhouetted
by the sliver of the waning crescent moon
reflected on the resting river.
They were honking and squawking
a noisy farewell that only lasted moments.
And then the night was quiet and cold again.
"Don't go," I whispered softly,
although I knew that this was
what they were meant to do.
It's just that I hate saying good-bye.
It always feels so lonely and so very final.

The Winds of March

The March wind is both fickle and whimsical.
It blusters its way through the still skeletal trees,
making the marsh grass shiver
as the river ripples in a rolling dance.
It bites and blisters the fragile snow drops
as they bravely reach for the sun.
And then, without warning,
it breathes a soft sigh,
caressing the seedlings with promise and hope.
Gently, it nudges the earth awake with unabashed affection.
The sea gulls swoop on their gliding ride,
and the swans seek shelter, weaving their knotty nests.

Nor'Easter

Even the geese are squawking
about this late autumn storm.
A Nor'Easter chugged up the curving coast,
churning the river into wild
whirlpools of frothing foam
which shattered the shoreline
spewing debris and black
river rocks into new homes.
The whining wind bent the birches
nearly to breaking,
as needles of rain shifted shape,
spinning into snowflakes.
Finally there was a single star
that scattered the clouds
and winked down upon the river,
and it breathed a sleepy promise
of a better morning.

Saturday Storm

The birds are still singing
in spite of the storm.
They are hidden somewhere safe
in the boughs of the evergreen
outside my window.
Unimpressed by winter's wrath,
they made the choice to stay here
all year long
with the precious promise
of spring
beating in their tiny hearts.

Sleet

Stinging shards of frozen glass are
tapping at my window.
Not yet rain but not still snow,
they hover in sparkling indecision.
My tiny birds still seek the solace of the feeders,
but even these intrepid travelers finally seek shelter
in the evergreens.
A storm with so many faces . . .
brilliant, crystalline needles of ice
stinging and scattering across the frozen ground,
deceptive miracles of magnificent danger.

Old Man Winter

The winter is feeling old and tired,
ragged around the edges.
Still able to throw a punch
but less willing to start the fight.
The wind more often whispers than whistles
and the darkness lessens its hold on the day.
There is a sort of promise in the still frigid air–
a harbinger of changes, soft and green
as the stained snow piles shrink in the sun.
There is a sense of slow awakening
from a dreamless depth of sleep;
an urge to stretch your roots,
breaking through the frozen earth
and reaching for the sun.

A Reflection

I close my eyes as the sun warms my face.
I appear to have weathered another winter.
I am older and sadder than I used to be,
staring at gaps where there were people;
gaps that widen until you could drown in them.
I'm often too much in the past to be present…
But the sun is my oldest friend,
and it works its magic on my storm-weary soul.
Within its soft buttery rays,
I am reminded that winter will most certainly end.
So I drink in the honey rays of promise.
We have been apart far too long this year.

The First Crocus

I saw it just this morning
as I pulled on my gloves against the cold;
a purple crocus, peeking shyly through the brown grass.
Tiny and perfect, it reached for the sun
and drank in the morning mist.
An intrepid warrior,
undaunted by the still bitter wind
and the frozen face of the sleeping earth,
it ignited the barren landscape
in its bravery and desire.
When I bent down to look more closely
I saw it was accompanied by friends.
These tenacious harbingers of springtime
made my heart ache with hope.

Lilac Time

It is such a short, sweet time when the lilacs bloom.

In all of their purple-plum pageantry,

they reassure us that May has once again taken root.

The scent of the lilac is far from subtle,

as I close my eyes and breathe in its heady perfume.

And suddenly memories cascade like the tiny flower buds.

The sheer joy of childhood in the spring,

of May baskets and processions, ribbons and reflections in

a profusion of petals locked in vases on the marble mantle piece.

My mother always mourned that lilacs disappeared before
Memorial Day,

in the same subtle, magical way they arrived,

offering their presence like old faithful friends to be savored and
shared

until it is time to move on.

Daffodils

I cannot be sad
in the presence of daffodils.
They offer too much hope.
Having weathered the winter,
they are born again.
Bundled in bulbs in the frozen ground,
they are undefeated by the icey shards
of wind-blown rain.
I'm not sure how they know the time
to lift their leaves upward
toward the still-chilly sky;
but somehow they do.
Their bright yellow faces
breathe in the springtime,
and they share their songs with me.

Palm Sunday, 2021

I'm painting stripes and splashing speckles on my Easter eggs.
Their smooth shape suggests that they have no beginning and
there is not an ending to be found.
This is a miracle of sorts,
a gracious gift to give or receive.
My paint brush skims their surface in happy, hopeful strokes,
and my winter weary soul senses a sort of promise in the swirling
spinning paint.
I'm well aware of their fragility, as they are aware of mine.
Once broken there is no repair.
So I place them carefully in a nest of soft spun grass,
and I offer a prayer to keep us safe in this not-so-gentle life

.

My Plants Love the Rain

This is a song of gratitude
for the gentle, nourishing rain
that coaxes my plants to smile.
They drink in the diamond droplets
that do not bend or even break
their fragile stems.
There is no unkind wind punishing and pummeling
their perfect petals.
They stretch toward the sky
and curl below the grass.
I know I am only their temporary keeper
as I weed and watch for each new bloom.
My plants rejoice in rainy celebration.
Stronger than I will ever be,
they share their little lives in a generous gesture,
soothing my soul as we sing in the rain.

Footprints — Near and Far

Pre-Dawn

The pre-dawn sky
holds a special sort of stillness.
The night slowly surrenders,
but the day has yet to arrive.
This is the time
when I search for my morning star,
the one that beams through the indigo shadows
and winks its way through my window.
I know this star has guided kings,
as well as weary mariners
heading towards the hearth's welcoming warmth.
And now it waits for me.
So I close my eyes and wish
for that twinkling peaceful pathway
that the morning star provides.

Starshine

Okay, I admit it.
I still love to whisper my wishes
to the star specks winking out at me
in the glossy, indigo sky.
Sometimes they listen;
more often they have plans of their own.
Nevertheless, I have faith I will find them
glimmering in incandescent warmth and light.
Believe me, I know
that I will burn out long before they do.

Evening Star

I used to find a dusky star
and claim it as my own beacon of brightness.
I closed my eyes and wished for
a continuation of my magic world.
But I don't do that anymore.
Now I know that the evening star
is not my reliable treasure.
It is fierce and fiery
and not inclined to listen.
It throbs its way through eons of
dust, debris and desire
blazing its way toward a trail of ending.
It is a raging reminder
that living is very tenuous and real.
It does not honor wishes.

Wind Chimes

The rustling of leaf skeletons in the wind
is a soft sound, barely a whisper.
It is a simple song, the sigh of the fairies,
so subtle, it could easily be missed.
But listen carefully because the melody is very brave.
The tenacious leaves cling to their branches
until they flutter back to the earth,
ready to nourish the winter roots
at the cost of their tiny, fragile lives.

A Single, Tenacious Chipmunk

In one sudden, startling moment
he leaps from the stone wall
to the leaf-covered mulch,
where the waxen holly bush used to live.
Pausing slightly, he wrinkles his nose,
breathing in the newly autumn air,
and then he is off again, skittering under the bushes
where the cool, earthy shadows await.
He curls himself into a contented sleep
until the darkness blankets the sun,
dreaming of a safe return home.

The Dragonfly

In a distant part of the field
where some ancient oaks loom large
and a tiny brook trickles past
a colony of dragonflies has a home,
hidden from the rest of the world.
Only if you look ever so carefully,
Will you see them as they lightly flutter and take in the sun.
Their wings are spun with silver see-through thread,
and in a moment of magic, they sparkle like sunbeams.
Their eyes are orbs of glass as they glance from side to side.
They are not quite mortal and not quite
magical, but somewhere in between;
ancient messengers from a primordial realm.
Consider yourself blessed if you spot one,
as it hesitantly hovers in a promise of peace.

Breakfast Time in Birdtown

It's breakfast time in Birdtown,
And everyone is here.
There's twittering and chirping
And squawking, loud and clear.
The mourning doves are standing guard
while their children flutter and hop.
The angry jays are pecking their way
as the seeds softly scatter and drop.
The chickadees prefer the deck,
much happier away from the crowd.
They're too polite to join the fight
Keeping their tiny heads bowed.
And then, suddenly, it's all over.
What is it that calls them away?
They leave in a pack, but I know
they'll be back.
They have so much to do in a day.

The Ways of the Jays

Three blue jays are in my feeder this morning
squawking and squabbling over sunflower seeds,
tapping and scratching their way to the bottom.
They are unpredictable and ever so cranky.
Their blue beauty is often ruffled
by their boisterous bickering.
They think nothing of swatting their sisters and brothers,
and their sharp chatter is endless.
My other bird friends stay away
until the jays are satisfied.
They are anxious, but avoid altercation.
Finally the blue feathered curmudgeons depart,
seeking shelter in the shadows of the pines.
The smaller birds breathe a sigh of relief, sharing tiny kernels
as a sense of peace returns.

Who is This?

Who is this tiny, timid bird
with his regal red head?
He visits alone, after the feeding frenzy is done.
He is patient and waits for his turn,
often accompanied by other feathered friends
who fly about scattering sunflower seeds far and wide.
I wonder what he does all day?
He seems to have a certain plan.
He flutters over from the chapel of the ancient pine
and disappears as quickly as he arrives.
Does he have shelter from the sudden storms
and the frigid nights?
I would like to spend a day with him;
two intrepid travelers searching for some sunshine.
We would look down on this weary world.
I would share the sky with my red-headed guide.

Footprints in the Snow

I see their footprints in the snow;
they are kindred spirits with the night.
Emerging from their cozy bowers, they forage for food,
greeting fellow wanderers in the frost filled moonlight.
Their days are spent sleeping in burrows lined with
last autumn's ancient leaves, twigs, and grasses,
but the night belongs to them.
In the solace of silence, they frolic by the river,
clambering up the rocks and sliding in the surf.
Dancing with their shadows, they glide along the moon path
until they are as exhausted as the night.
Then they wind their way home, to be welcomed
by the ever gentle Mother Earth until the dark descends again.

Race Point
A Walk to the Edge of My World

The clouds had gathered back at home
But on the beach, the sun was strong
and the sky was so brilliantly blue.
Frank and I were walking to the edge of the land,
a magical, mystical place where earth joins ocean.
The gulls walked with us
completely at ease with these interlopers in their space.
They wrapped us in their harmony, asking nothing but respect.
And we were happy to agree, treading lightly on the sand,
leaving footprints that disappeared behind us,
conscious that we were guests.
We were offered something so special,
a chance to share what had been here long before we arrived,
and would remain long after we were gone.
Ahead of us lay a blanket of cerulean blue,
stretching as far as a dream might.
What can you say in the face of such magnificence?
Thank you, thank you, thank you . . .

Hewitt Pond, Raynham

When I was walking
through the storm-battered woods,
the softly blurred swirls of rain-ruined leaves
began to speak of their final, fractured journey toward the end.
Yes, they lingered just a little too long,
proudly strutting across the glimmering, golden stage.
Finally, the furious, fiery russet reds
have taken one last bow
and drifted toward the earth's embrace.
They tell me that this is what they were born to do,
as they hunker down into a magnificent mash to feed the soil,
plumping tiny seeds and slender
roots until they break through
their blanket and stretch toward the sky.
"But this won't happen for a while," they warn.
"It is time to rest and the calming
cold will lull us to sleep."
"Depend on it," they whisper.
And then,
I am alone again.

Abandoned Railroad Tracks Sweets Knoll

The wooden planks are covered with moss.
My feet crunch down on the crinkled brown leaves.
There is water on either side of me
and mudflats, dark and glistening in the early spring sun.
I follow a route a train once traveled through marsh and swamp
along the tangled Taunton River.
Where it chugged away from
or to where it was going.
Only the worn path can testify,
and it is holding fast its secrets.
But trains are so very magical
puffing their songs that signal leaving.
When I get to the broken bridge,
it is half swept away,
the victim of too many winters.
I won't tempt fate by crossing.
My feet know better than that.
I'll let the mystery of the other side
lure me back on another day.

Lake Kanasatka

No one had to tell me to tread lightly;
I knew it in my heart.
This path did not belong to me,
but it opened up for sharing.
It was wealthy in twigs and leaves and wooden bridges.
It scurried and bounced over moss-covered rocks,
through the blackened ruins of a camp fire,
past a brook that was laughing its way to the lake,
until it kissed the sparkles of sand.
The path gave itself to me without fear or reservation.
It told me to listen for the loons,
to take deep and blessed breaths of the purifying breeze.
It coursed through my body of clay, seeping into my much
bruised soul.
Of course, this gift was temporary, as everything really is.
Chaos and worry awaited my return.
But I was stronger than before,
knowing that the path would welcome me
for as long as I allowed myself to be led.

A New York Poem #1

What has happened to my city?
I am walking among the ghosts.
There are for rent signs on buildings,
shuttered and sad.
Paper covered windows hide
chairs placed on tables,
and a wind ripples through the
lonely, littered courtyards,
as trash skitters across the street.
My city has always been overflowing
with dreams, plans and promises.
Where has it all gone?
Now cloudy, sullen and sickly
the city that never sleeps
has closed its tired eyes.
It no longer belongs to me.

Dancing in the Street
A New York Poem #2

She is a most welcome, uplifting sight,
gliding gracefully in the crosswalk.
Tall and lithe, she waves her hands toward heaven,
her tattered skirt swaying against her hips.
She is well known on this street, and the traffic slides around her.
Her dance is filled with joy,
a daily rythmic prayer.
She weaves her way through the seasons,
bare feet leaping in faith.
But she only dances until it is dark,
and then she is gone,
only to return tomorrow.

The Lady with a Walker
A New York Poem #3

The lady with the walker is here again.
Taking tiny bits of her bagel, she feeds the pigeons,
who seem to know her well.
She sneaks a cigarette on the sly
as she gulps a styrofoam cup of coffee.
Although it is muggy and still this morning,
She hugs her black sweater.
Soon, she will go back inside,
leaving bagel crumbs and cigarette butts
on the pavement.

The Beginning of the End of the Beginning

Grief

Your late night visit
was completely unexpected.
But you needed no invitation
and ignored my other plans.
How does it feel to be the guest
no one wants to entertain?
You have made yourself comfortable
in your dark traveling suit.
You have taken up residence in my heart,
letting me know you have no plans for
departing anytime soon.

It All Fell Apart

A lifetime of precious, magical memories
was swept away so quickly
as the Tsunami struck our lives.
Suddenly, there are only memories,
and the line disappears beween pleasure and pain.
What kind of world is this
to provide us with the tools to create a life of wonder,
only to destroy it in an everlasting whim?

The Year of Firsts

The year of firsts following a death,
is like no other time,
except, perhaps, the year of birth.
We joyously celebrate first birthdays,
first anniversaries, first holidays, first season change.
But then we drift from wonder to hunger,
to apprehension and, ultimately, to pain.
The memories gently move from sweet to bitter,
to bittersweet,
unsure if they are a blessing or a curse.

These Days . . .

I'm thinking of those
who always try
yet face such frequent failure.
And then there are the smug,
self-styled victors,
who viciously smash the spoils.
Kindness becomes the stuff
of fairy tales,
while happily ever after
heads for the hills.
This is when
my soul sighs
and my heart hurts,
trying to rationalize reality.

November 29th

And so, another dream has gone rogue;
Re-emerging as simply a memory.
Was it finished with me?
Was I finished with it?
Defining dreams does not work out so well.
They are better left within.
When they disappear, they don't return.
Could something still be waiting in the wings,
a ghost of a grain of a plan?
Might it take root and spread out?
Perhaps the next one will be a dream come true.

Shadows

A shadow lives
in the home of two souls who travelled together;
a smokey, silent shape of what was once substance
but will not be real again.
These shadows appear in the sunlight
as well as the darkness,
slowly shape shifting to suit any image, any time.

Chinna

She is a darting shadow of who she was,
proving that great love will cause great pain.
She makes her way through a misty forest of memory,
and the shifting shapes offer comfort and peace
of that tender time before,
when the fabric of her life
was a vivid weave of joy.
I try to go with her,
but these memories do not belong to me.
I am still in the present;
she is gently cradling the past.
But I will always try to walk with her.
I would do anything to ease her pain.
But I can only be by her side,
as we take one step at a time
through this frightening, most fragile forest.

Morning Sounds

The reassuring sound of footsteps,
the sharp snap of the coffeemaker,
the stream of steam from the shower;
don't take the morning sounds for granted.
Roll yourself up in the sounds that scatter sleep.
There will someday be an empty time;
and whenever it comes,
it will be far too soon and sudden.
It will be a silence that echoes loudly,
punctuated by a pain that will not be denied.

The Other Daughters

"The other daughters," that's what she
always called us,
so interested in our plans and dreams,
filling us with food made with lemons and love.
We wanted to be around her
because she saw the best within us
and was unfazed by our many imperfections.
Now I see her sparkle in her daughter's bright eyes
as they fill with grief and gratitude.
She is just like her mother,
nurturing, gentle and kind.
What a magnificent gift
has been left for us all.

The Other Side

The other side of sunshine
owns the shadowy, echoing absence
of comfort and warmth.
There is a fractured fall apart
of everything familiar and prized.
This is a strange, unwelcoming,
barren country.
Even though bittersweet memories
stoke glowing embers of lost yesterdays,
there is no warmth,
and the day stretches ahead endlessly.

Chinna + the Leaves

"I have to keep up with these falling leaves,"
she said, pushing back an errant strand of hair.
"I'll need to be out here all day, surely into the dark."
And I know she is thinking
that is the loneliest time;
when the wood fires are burning
and her neighbors' houses are warm and welcoming.
She has lost her place in that world.
So she relentlessly rakes though
her hands are stiff with cold.
She knows she won't warm up if she goes inside.
The chill of being alone is so much stronger.
So she pushes the leaves into neat little piles
as my heart breaks for her.

Endings

Endings bring beginnings.
Beginnings always have an end.
Everything new loses its shine
until it finally is old.
What begins as joy ends in sorrow,
and sorrow triggers memories,
going back to the beginning
on a final journey to the end.

Now I Know . . .

Now I know about sadness.
I know that it spreads softly,
puddling in painful pools.
Oh, yes. Now I know—
what I will never be able to understand,
much less explain.
And when I am drowning in those dark waters,
there is no comfort to be found,
no chance to turn back,
nothing to be spared.
Now I know . . .
Now I know . . .

5 Important Questions Without Answers

Why do terrible, unimaginable things happen?

Is suffering anyone's fault?

Why are we inevitably, completely alone in the end?

Is there anything else?

How can something be bitter and sweet simultaneously?

The Greatest Beauty

And yet, there is still great beauty.
The sun rises in the changing violet sky.
The river water glistens, embracing smooth, time-rounded rocks.
The birds welcome the daylight
reveling in rain as well as warmth.
And the wild flowers–
they open up to drink the dew on their perfect petals.
I can hear the wind chimes whisper
that the day ahead is an unpainted canvas.
Yes, it is too true that many unchangeable
changes may occur before the twilight time.
Some will be subtle and slight.
Others so very permanent.
The night will close our weary, worried eyes,
and the day will end, transforming itself
into another precious sunrise.
There is no greater gift.

The End

Made in the USA
Middletown, DE
17 September 2022

10058116R00073